ANIMAL SUPERPOWERS

RATS
Biting Through Concrete!

Emma Carlson Berne

PowerKiDS
press
New York

Published in 2014 by The Rosen Publishing Group, Inc.
29 East 21st Street, New York, NY 10010

First Edition

Editor: Joanne Randolph
Book Design: Kate Vlachos

Photo Credits: Cover Scott Tilley/Oxford Scientific/Getty Images; pp. 4–5 Graham Taylor/Shutterstock.com; p. 6 Tom McHugh/Photo Researchers/Getty Images; p. 7 (sidebar) Maslov Dmitry/Shutterstock.com; pp. 7, 9 Heiko Kiera/Shutterstock.com; p. 8 © iStockphoto.com/Liz Leyden; p. 10 Oshchepkov Dmitry/Shutterstock.com; p. 11 David Lees/Digital Vision/Getty Images; pp. 12–13 Paul Broadbent/Shutterstock.com; p. 14 Nature Picture Library/Britain On View/Getty Images; p. 15 Polina Truver/Shutterstock.com; p. 16 Stephen McSweeny/Shutterstock.com; p. 17 Eric Gevaert/Shutterstock.com; p. 18 John Cancalosi/Peter Arnold/Getty Images; p. 19 Gisela Delpho/Picture Press/Getty Images; p. 20 (sidebar) Pakhnyushcha/Shutterstock.com; pp. 20–21 E.A. Janes/age fotostock/Getty Images; p. 22 annedde/E+/Getty Images.
Interactive eBook Only: pp. 4, 6 Discovery FootageSource/Getty Images; p. 8 Serguei Liachenko/iStockfootage/Getty Images; p. 10 GK Hart-Vikki Hart/Image Bank Film/Getty Images; p. 11 Energy Films Library/Image Bank Film/Getty Images; p. 15 sarot/iStockfootage/Getty Images; p. 17 Stu Porter/Shutterstock.com; p. 21 Heiko Kiera/Shutterstock.com.

Library of Congress Cataloging-in-Publication Data

Berne, Emma Carlson.
 Rats : biting through concrete! / by Emma Carlson Berne. — 1st ed.
     p. cm. — (Animal superpowers)
 Includes index.
 ISBN 978-1-4777-0752-4 (library binding) — ISBN 978-1-4777-0845-3 (pbk.) —
 ISBN 978-1-4777-0846-0 (6-pack)
 1. Rats—Juvenile literature. I. Title.
 QL737.R666B47 2014
 599.35'2—dc23
                                    2012049056

Manufactured in the United States of America

CPSIA Compliance Information: Batch #S13PK6: For Further Information contact Rosen Publishing, New York, New York at 1-800-237-9932

Contents

Rats! 4

Remarkable Rodents.......................................6

Where Rats Live 8

Smart and Friendly......................................10

Facts About Rats 12

Eating Everything..14

Danger! 16

A Rat's Life 18

Growing Up as a Rat 20

A Part of Our World 22

Glossary...23

Index 24

Websites 24

Rats!

"Rats!" you might say if you forgot your homework. A character in an old movie might exclaim, "You dirty rat!" Many people think of disease, dirtiness, or sneakiness when they think of rats. Throughout history, people have often trapped and killed rats. Not many people would think of them as having superpowers.

Rats are actually extremely intelligent, clever, and clean **rodents**. They can **adapt** to nearly any environment. Rats take good care of their babies and live in large social groups. Pet rats love interacting with humans. They like to be cuddled and can even play games like tug-of-war and peekaboo. Let's learn more about these smart, superpowered animals.

Rats are omnivores. This means they will eat most anything, including seeds, grains, fruit, bugs, and even people's garbage.

Remarkable Rodents

There are more than 100 different **species** of rats. The Norway rat, which is also called the brown rat, is the species most people are familiar with.

The world is full of many other kinds of rats. The packrat, or wood rat, for instance, is known for carrying interesting objects off to its burrow.

The desert wood rat lives in the deserts of western North America. It eats beans, mesquite and juniper leaves, and parts of cacti, among other things.

SUPER TEETH

Rats have amazingly strong teeth. They can put 24,000 pounds per square inch (1,687 kg/sq cm) of pressure on whatever they are chewing. This is enough pressure to chew through wood, soft metal like lead, plaster, and even concrete, like cinder blocks.

The kangaroo rat can hop long distances on its big back legs. In South America, the spiny rat has bristly fur to keep **predators** from eating it. The largest rat in the world is the African giant pouched rat. Including its tail, it can be 3 feet (1 m) long!

The brown rat is one of the most common kinds of rats. It lives on every continent except Antarctica. It is the most successful mammal on the planet, second only to people.

7

Where Rats Live

Rats live anywhere there is a food source. Rats love people's leftovers, so they often live near people in cities and towns.

You are out in New York City. Suddenly, you see a little brown form scurry across an alleyway. It's a rat!

Some species of rats, like the African giant pouched rat and the spiny rat, live in tropical forests. Most wild rats live near people, though, in order to eat their food waste.

Rats may live in forests, fields, deserts, or pretty much anywhere.

In cities and suburbs, rats live in the walls of buildings, in sewers, or in basements. In the country, they might live in farmers' fields, where they eat leftover grain. They can stow away on ships and hitchhike rides in trucks. In fact, rats can live almost anywhere in the world that people live.

Smart and Friendly

People are used to thinking of dogs or chimps as smart animals. How about rats, though? In fact, rats are extremely intelligent. Pet rats can play all sorts of games, including hide-and-seek, wrestling, and tag. They can be taught tricks and can come when their names are called.

Rats often live in groups. Animals that live in groups are called social animals. People are social animals, too!

Because rats are friendly and smart, they can make great pets.

Rats also are affectionate and social. They live in large groups in the wild. They sleep piled up on top of each other and spend a lot of time grooming and licking each other. Pet rats like to be held and will even try to groom their owners.

FACTS ABOUT RATS

1 Rat burrows have three or four entrances and separate rooms for food storage, sleeping, and going to the bathroom. They even have emergency exits!

2 When they are grooming themselves, rats sometimes use their back toenails as combs.

3 Rats can spread diseases to humans. Infected fleas that live on rats can jump onto humans and bite them, spreading the illness.

4 The kangaroo rat doesn't need to drink water. It eats seeds instead and then makes its own water from the starches in the seeds.

5 Scientists often use rats for experiments. More than 90 percent of all animals in **laboratories** are rats.

6 Rats are good climbers, jumpers, and diggers. The brown rat can jump a 4-foot (1 m) wall. Brown rats can even swim.

Eating Everything

Rats are **omnivores** and can eat an amazing range of food. In the wild, rats will **scavenge** for plants, seeds, nuts, grain, insects, worms, and eggs of all kinds. They will eat dead animals and will hunt and kill mice, small lizards and snakes, frogs and toads, and birds. They can even catch fish with their paws.

Farmers consider rats pests because they enter grain storage places and eat a lot of grain.

Rats that live near people will often invade garbage cans and feast on leftover food scraps, from french fries to rotting bananas. On farms, they will eat spilled grain or clean up the corn or wheat left in the field after the harvest.

Rats will eat whatever they can find. This rat is feasting on a piece of watermelon it has found in a person's garbage.

Danger!

If a rat sees a shadow fall over its body, it had best run for cover. A hawk such as this one may be swooping in to make it a meal.

Rats are very **vulnerable** to predators. Out in the wild, rats are hunted and eaten by medium-sized mammals such as foxes, weasels, skunks, and coyotes. **Birds of prey**, like owls and hawks, can easily swoop down and pluck a rat from a field. Large snakes often swallow rats whole.

Dogs are another source of danger to rats. Some breeds, like the rat terrier, were bred specifically to hunt and kill these rodents. Do you know the other main enemy of rats? For centuries, all over the world, rats have been trapped, poisoned, and hunted by people who don't want them living so close.

An African wild dog has caught a rat for its dinner.

A Rat's Life

Like many small rodents, rats have short lives and lots of babies. A female rat is **pregnant** for about 21 days. Then she will have a **litter** of anywhere from 2 to 14 babies. In only 14 days, the little rats start eating food, and in just about two months, they can have babies of their own. Some rats can have more than 100 babies in just one year!

This is a whitethroat wood rat nest. Wood rats are often called packrats due to their habit of collecting sticks, pinecones, and other matter and bringing it back to their nests.

Rats will huddle with their family groups in the nest.

Rats don't live very long, especially in the wild. Most of them are eaten by predators within one or two years. Healthy pet rats can live longer, up to three or even five years.

Growing Up as a Rat

A pregnant rat mother will make a soft nest for her babies, using grass, rags, shredded paper, or any other soft material she can find. When rat babies are born, they are blind and furless, and can barely move. They can squirm over to their mother to **nurse**, though.

The babies will drink milk from their mothers for about six weeks. However, within just two weeks, they will begin watching their mother to learn what foods are good to eat.

EVER-GROWING TEETH

Like all rodents, rats have four **incisors** in the front of their mouths that are excellent for chewing. In fact, rats have to chew because their teeth grow all the time. If they didn't keep them worn down, a rat's teeth would grow about 4 to 5 inches (10–13 cm) a year.

Baby rats are helpless when they are first born. In a few weeks, though, they will be ready to leave the nest with their mother.

21

A Part of Our World

Rats and people have lived together for many centuries. Many people consider rats to be **pests**. Rats can carry diseases that they can give to people. They eat farmers' crops. They chew holes in house wires and insulation.

Rats are also very useful to people, though. Scientists use rats to study drugs and diseases that can later help humans. For better or for worse, rats will probably always be a part of our world.

Rats are bred for medical use. Scientists have been able to help countless sick people based on what they have learned from rats. We owe these smart animals a thank you.

Glossary

adapt (uh-DAPT) To change to fit requirements.

birds of prey (BURDZ UV PRAY) Birds that hunt live animals for food.

incisors (in-SY-zurz) An animal's four front teeth used for cutting.

laboratories (LA-bruh-tor-eez) Rooms in which scientists do tests.

litter (LIH-ter) A group of animals born to the same mother at the same time.

nurse (NURS) When a female feeds her baby milk from her body.

omnivores (OM-nih-vorz) Animals that eat both plants and animals.

pests (PESTS) Plants or animals that hurt people.

predators (PREH-duh-terz) Animals that kill other animals for food.

pregnant (PREG-nent) When a female has a baby or babies growing inside her.

rodents (ROH-dents) Animals with gnawing teeth, such as mice.

scavenge (SKA-venj) To search for and collect certain items.

species (SPEE-sheez) One kind of living thing. All people are one species.

vulnerable (VUL-neh-ruh-bel) Open to attack or harm.

Index

A
African giant pouched rat, 7–8

B
babies, 4, 18, 20
brown rat(s), 6, 13
burrow, 6

D
disease(s), 4, 12, 22

F
foxes, 16

G
games, 4, 10
grain, 9, 14–15

H
humans, 4, 13, 22

K
kangaroo rat, 7, 13

N
New York City, 8
Norway rat, 6

O
omnivores, 14

P
people, 4, 6, 8–10, 15, 17, 22
pests, 22
predators, 7, 16, 19

R
rat terrier, 17
rodents, 4, 6, 17–18, 20

S
sewers, 9
skunks, 16
South America, 7
species, 6, 8
spiny rat, 7–8
superpowers, 4

T
tail, 7

W
weasels, 16

Websites

Due to the changing nature of Internet links, PowerKids Press has developed an online list of websites related to the subject of this book. This site is updated regularly. Please use this link to access the list:
www.powerkidslinks.com/asp/rat/